# Bert's Boat

**Tony Mitton**

**Illustrated by Sholto Walker**

RIGBY

This is the boat that Bert built.

This is Bert's boat.

It bobs on the waves.

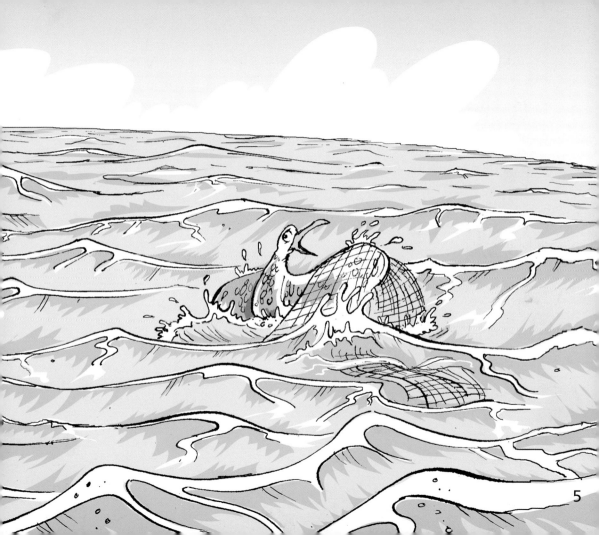

This is the bird Bert
quickly saves.

This is a cliff
with deep, dark caves.

9

This is a box
that sits on the rocks.

This is the key
that opens the box.

And this is the gold
that Bert unlocks.

Bert and the bird,
afloat on their boat.